STUFFED

With

MAD

Written by Frank Jacobs

Illustrated by Bob Clarke

WARNER BOOKS

A Warner Communications Company

MENU

5

A **MAD** Look at Gourmets

In a French Restaurant

Waiter, I'll begin with the **lobster cocktail,** then for the soup I'll have the **vichysoisse!**

For the **entree** I'll try the **Chateaubriand** with **bearnaise sauce,** the **asparagus Hollandaise** and the **lyonnaise potatoes** with a **roquefort salad!**

9

At an Expensive Lunch

In a Suburban Home

In a Far-Off Country

In a Very Fancy Restaurant

17

In a Japanese Restaurant

21

22

At a Chinese Restaurant

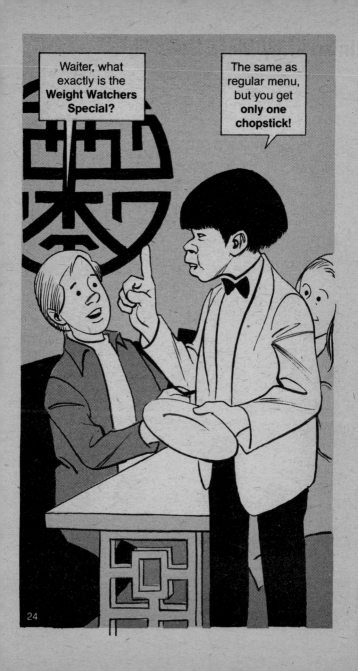

In an Army Mess Hall

You Know You're a Junkfood Junkie

You know you're a Junkfood Junkie…

…when you prowl the streets at two in
the morning looking for an all-night bakery.

You know you're a Junkfood Junkie...

...when you sprinkle powdered sugar on top of Hershey bars.

…when you show withdrawal symptoms after
two days without a jelly doughnut.

…when you lick the insides of
empty ice-cream cartons.

…when you throw a tantrum after finding
out your supermarket is out of Oreos.

...when you pay overweight charges on
a plane so you can take along a
suitcase full of brownies.

You know you're a Junkfood Junkie...

...when you have a charge account at
the neighborhood candy store.

You know you're a Junkfood Junkie...

...when you lock yourself in a room
and take sugar intravenously.

You know you're a Junkfood Junkie...

...when you keep cheesecake on your
night-table in case you get hungry in your sleep.

...when you take a sledge-hammer to the candy-bar machine after it swallows your last quarter.

THE EDIBLE MOTHER GOOSE

Humpty Dumpty

Humpty Dumpty sat on a wall;
Humpty Dumpty died in a fall;

That night the chef served the king
and the queen
The biggest damn omelet
they ever had seen!

Sing A Song Of Sixpence

Sing a song of sixpence,
A pocket full of rye;
Four-and-twenty blackbirds
Baked in a pie.

When the pie was opened,
The king let out a squeal,
And promptly hanged the chef
For making such a yecchy meal.

Old Mother Hubbard

Old Mother Hubbard
Went into her cupboard
To get her poor dog a Sauterne;
The dog said, "Good grief!
"I am dining on beef,
"And the wine should be red—can't you learn?"

As I Was Going To St. Ives

As I was going to St. Ives,
I had a bowl of soup with chives,
Three macaroons, a turkey leg,
Six Twinkies and a scrambled egg,
A pound of peanuts from a can,
A dish of prunes with Raisin Bran,
Five ears of corn, a pan-fried steak,
Four Pepsis and a birthday cake,
Two candied yams, a lemon ice,
And seven plates of pork fried rice;

How many minutes went by before I got heartburn and nausea and indigestion and nearly passed out on the road to St. Ives?

Mary Had A Little Calf

Mary had a little calf
    Of which she was quite proud;
And ev'rywhere that Mary went
    She gathered quite a crowd.

She fed the calf with loving care,
    Just like a dog or cat;
And from the portions that it ate,
    The calf grew big and fat.

55

Mary has no calf today,
　　But this we will reveal;
Inside her freezer you will find
　　A month's supply of veal.

Solomon Grundy

Solomon Grundy
Had turkey on Monday,
A side of beef Tuesday,
Lasagna on Wednesday,
A pot roast on Thursday,
Stewed chicken on Friday,
A veal shank on Saturday,
The leftovers Sunday;
So much for the diet
Of Solomon Grundy.

MAD

about

ALPHABET SOUP

DELEGATES DINING ROO

In an Athens Cafe

In Philadelphia in 1776

68

In a Modern American Restaurant

A PREHISTORIC FOOD TALE

Good News

& Bad News

GOOD NEWS is being invited to a gourmet's house for dinner.

BAD NEWS is discovering that he's on a meatless, sauceless, sweetless, flavorless diet.

81

GOOD NEWS is being careful not to drink the water during a vacation in Mexico.

BAD NEWS is that it doesn't
  make any difference.

GOOD NEWS is ordering a steak in the language of the foreign country that you're visiting.

BAD NEWS is finding out that you'll never be a linguist.

GOOD NEWS is discovering a yummy, exotic dish in a small East Indian restaurant.

BAD NEWS is discovering
what you've been eating.

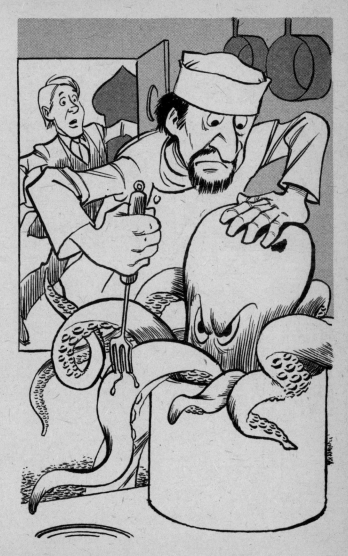

GOOD NEWS is a meal in a
highly rated restaurant.

BAD NEWS is the waiter saying that he thinks they're out of the Special.

GOOD NEWS is the waiter
discovering that there
is one Special left.

BAD NEWS is tasting the Special and wishing the waiter had been right in the first place.

One Day In Outer Space

94

If Great Poets Wrote About Food

The Diner's Lament
as by Walt Whitman

O Waiter! My Waiter!
I've tried to get your eye,
And though I've called, and waved, and yelled,
you always pass me by;

My stomach growls, my mouth is parched,
 I sit in desperation;
But your response to me remains:
 "I'm sorry, not my station."

O Waiter! My Waiter!
Do I look cheap, perchance?
I promise that I'll tip you well;
I'll pay it in advance;

I pledge that I'll forget for good
this worst of persecutions;
I'll even shrug my shoulders when
you say, "No substitutions."

O Waiter! My Waiter!
Some food I beg of you!
A slice of bread, a roll, a scrap
of melba toast will do;

Praise be! At last! You've come to me
with stature so imposing;
How good of you to let me know
the restaurant is closing.

Fast-food Hiawatha
as by Longfellow

In a brownstone in Manhattan
Lived the lean one, Hiawatha;
As a cook he was a failure,
And he came to hate his kitchen,
For he failed at every task there,
Failed at toasting bread for breakfast,

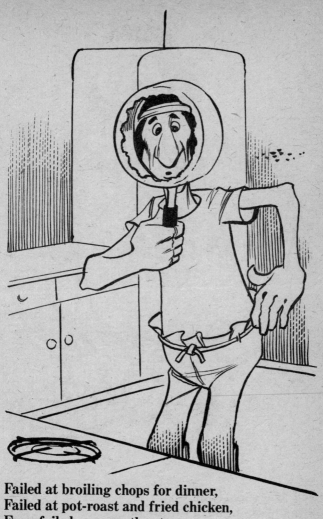

Failed at broiling chops for dinner,
Failed at pot-roast and fried chicken,
Even failed, so goes the story,
When he tried to boil water;
Quite a klutz when in the kitchen
Was the lean one, Hiawatha.

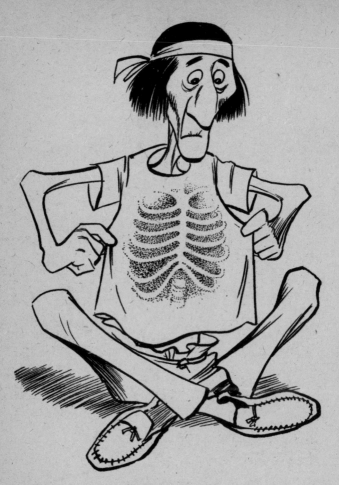

Sad to see was Hiawatha
From his failures in the kitchen,
And his face grew gaunt and ghastly,
And his frame was racked by hunger,
And his ribs showed through his T-shirt,
And his body weight diminished

Till a skeleton he looked like,
And when friends came by to see him,
They were shocked by his appearance,
Muttered sentiments of pity,
And remarked to Hiawatha
That he looked like death warmed over.

"This won't do," said Hiawatha,
After days of near-starvation,
And he rose up like the corn-stalk,
Staggered out into the sunlight,
Scorning passersby who mocked him,
And he wobbled down the sidewalk
Searching for some quick solution

110

To the hunger pains that racked him,
To the gnawing in his stomach,
And he stopped, all of a sudden,
For beyond him, in the distance,
Loomed the answer to his troubles:
Filled with hopes and dreams and hunger
Was the lean one, Hiawatha.

"What is this?" cried Hiawatha,
As he scanned the sight before him,
Which was filled with fast food shops there,
Selling goodies in abundance,
And he yearned and salivated
For the chicken from Kentucky,

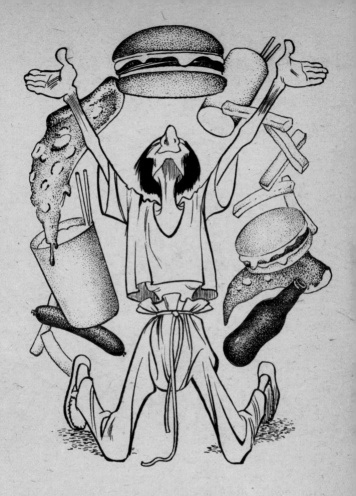

For the Big Mac at MacDonald's,
For the Burger King's great Whopper,
For the Pizza Hut and Wendy's,
For the Dairy Queen and Gino's,
And he thanked his God in heaven
For the blessings all around him.

How he ate, did Hiawatha,
At the fast-food shops around him,
Ate two thighs and seven drumsticks
Of the chicken from Kentucky,
Ate four Big Macs with raw onions
From the counter of MacDonald's,
Ate the Burger King's great Whopper,

Drank the Dairy Queen's thick malted,
Not to mention cheesy slices
From the Pizza Hut and Gino's
And a large-size Coca-Cola
With a plate of fries from Wendy's;
Soon revived and feeling better
Was the lean one, Hiawatha.

How he thrived, did Hiawatha,
On the fast foods he discovered;
Seven days a week he dined there,
Packing in the fries and burgers,
And no ribs showed through his T-shirt,
And his Levi's did not fit him,
And his body weight did double,

And his face grew round and bloated;
Warned his doctor, "Hiawatha,
You are fat, which is a danger
To your health, which now is shaky;"
But unheeding of this peril,
Unconcerned with his condition
Was the fat one, Hiawatha.

For a year did Hiawatha
Stuff himself with fries and burgers
(Also cakes and Cokes and malteds,
Thighs and drumsticks, pies of pizza),
Till one day, as was predicted,
He awoke one cloudy morning,

Tried to rise but found his body
Could do nothing but just lie there;
And afraid was Hiawatha
Of his death which loomed before him;
And he wished, did Hiawatha,
That he'd listened to his doctor.

It was then that he remembered
He had dreamed a dream prophetic;
'Twas a vision of nirvana,
And at once his gloom did vanish,
And at peace was Hiawatha,
Unafraid was Hiawatha,
Full of joy was Hiawatha,
Undismayed was Hiawatha,
For he knew, did Hiawatha,
As his final breath was taking,
Though this world he was departing,
There were fast-food shops in heaven.

Half-baked Jabberwocky

as by Lewis Carroll

'Twas basil and the spicy cloves
    Did chive and chutney in the greens;
All mango were the carrot loaves
    And likewise franks and beans.

"Beware the Artichoke, my son!
  The leek that prawns, the lox of hash,
Beware the escarole and shun
  The deadly succotash!"

He took his marzipan in thyme,
  His rutabaga in soufflés,
Then truffled by the lemon-lime,
  And muttered, "Mayonnaise."

And while in mushroom thought he sat,
    The Artichoke, with chard of quince,
Came waffling through the chicken-fat
    And dropped a cherry blintz.

Fondue! Fondue! And goulash, too,
   The marzipan the foe did squash;
He left it cress, a kipper mess
   And scalloped home to wash.

"And did thou dill the Artichoke?
    Come kale with me and barbecue!
O candied yam! O chowdered clam!"
    He curried in his stew.

'Twas basil and the spicy cloves
 Did chive and chutney in the greens;
All mango were the carrot loaves
 And likewise franks and beans.

The Dieter's "IF"
as by Rudyard Kipling

If you can nix the pie and go for sherbet,
And make your friends believe you're satisfied;

If you've a yen for cheesecake and can curb it,
And not admit a part of you has died;

If you can eat the meat but not the noodles,
And not go slightly crazy when you do;

If you can pass a plate of apple strudels,
Without the need to have "a taste or two;"

If you can skip the tasty crab au gratin,
And not lament the joy you surely missed;

If you can swear off bread and not feel rotten,

While half of you cries, "Dummy, why resist?"

If you've the will for sticking with this diet,
And somehow all these yummy things avoid,
Don't tell me that you're human—I won't buy it;
'Cause, man, you gotta be some kind of droid.

Sugar as by William Blake

Sugar! Sugar, gleaming white,
On my table, day and night,
Is it not a dreadful shame
Dieticians smirch thy name?

Sugar! Sugar, pleasing me
In my coffee and my tea;
Hark not to the speech of boobs;
Thank, you, yes, I'll have three cubes.

Sugar! Sugar, sweet to take,
Friend of pudding, pal of cake;
Critics hope you'll be replaced;
Could it be they lack your taste?

Sugar! Sugar, flowing proud,
Target of the health-food crowd;
What inspires these slurs unkind?
Could it be you're too refined?

139

Broccoli as by Joyce Kilmer

I think that I shall never see
Hot choc'late sauce on broccoli;
But if I do, I give my word
I'll have two plates, but not a third.

Get Stuffed With Shakespeare

...black as hell, as dark as night!
"Sonnets"
This was the most unkindest cut of all!
"Julius Caesar" Act III, Scene 5

149

151

MADDITIONS

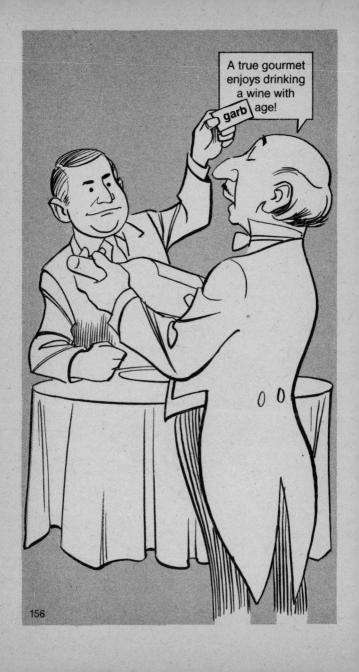

157

158

159

What They Say

and

What They Mean

What they say

What they mean

What they say

What they mean

What they say

What they mean

164

What they say

What they mean

What they say

What they mean

What they say

What they mean

What they say

What they mean

What they say

What they mean

What they say

What they mean

171

172

One Day Long Ago In
BIBLICAL TIMES

175

CAMP-OUT COOKERY

183

184

185

And now we come to the end! Not just the **end of this book,** but the **end of all of us!** Be glad you've survived long enough to gulp down these—

EPITAPHS
FOR
EATERS

HENRY
FARDOON
1924 ~ 1975

WILD MUSHROOMS
HENRY SOUGHT;
ATE A GOOD ONE ~
SO HE THOUGHT.

FRED
GRUNION
1934-1980

CHOKED FOR GOOD
DINING OUT;
NEXT TIME, FRED,
BONE YOUR TROUT.

LEON
DRINGLE
1920-1977

WOULDN'T DIET;
WOULDN'T FAST;
HERE LIES LEON,
THIN AT LAST.

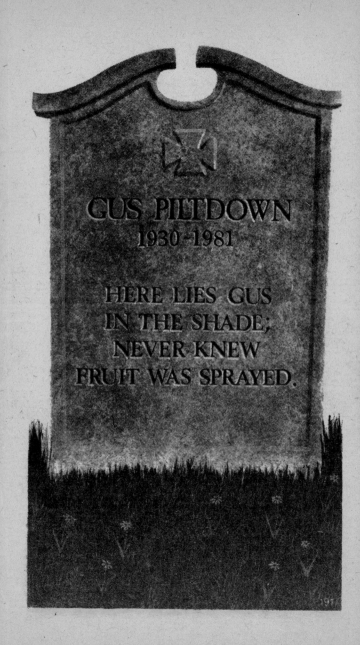

SY RUMPLEMAN
1922~1979

SY ATE PORK
IN JULY;
PORK TOO RARE;
BYE~BYE, SY.